Absolute Cr

The Trail's End

The Story of Bonnie and Clyde

ABSOLUTE CRIME

By Wallace Edwards

Absolute Crime Books

www.absolutecrime.com

© 2013. All Rights Reserved.

Table of Contents

ABOUT US 3

INTRODUCTION 4

CHAPTER 1: A LOVE BIGGER THAN TEXAS 9

CHAPTER 2: INCARCERATION 19

CHAPTER 3: EARLY MISADVENTURES AND MURDERS 30

CHAPTER 4: BUCK JOINS THE BARROW GANG 45

CHAPTER 5: PLATTE CITY WAKEUP CALL 67

CHAPTER 6: DEXFIELD PARK 88

CHAPTER 7: THE FINAL RUN 98

CHAPTER 8: DEATH AND LEGACY 107

CONCLUSION 114

BIBLIOGRAPHY 117

About Us

Absolute Crime publishes only the best true crime literature. Our focus is on the crimes that you've probably never heard of, but you are fascinated to read more about. With each engaging and gripping story, we try to let readers relive moments in history that some people have tried to forget.

Remember, our books are not meant for the faint at heart. We don't hold back—if a crime is bloody, we let the words splatter across the page so you can experience the crime in the most horrifying way!

If you enjoy this book, please visit our homepage to see other books we offer; if you have any feedback, we'd love to hear from you!

Introduction

At the edge of a pond on a north-central Texas farm, a cottonmouth slithered into the water and started gliding furtively across the surface in search of prey. A chorus of birds whistled in the overhanging trees, the branches reflecting in the still water. There among the leafy shadows, the hungry reptile zigzagged along, leaving murky green ripples in its wake.

There were three ponds on this family farm in Tarrant County, and Delbert Coons, the oldest of six kids, tramped through the field toward the pond closest to Norwood Road. One of the family's two workhorses clomped alongside him. Delbert held the lead rope loosely in one hand as he led the horse to the pond for a much needed drink.

He and his siblings often swam in the big pond; in fact, that's where they bathed during the scorching summer months. Like many other families in the early 1930s, the Coons didn't have electricity. During winter, if they wanted warm bath water, they heated it in a big iron caldron outside their farm house on a fire whose flames shot four or five feet into the air. They didn't have a phone either. If they needed one, they drove into Bedford to use the phone at the Fitch Store. Due to the desperate effects of the Great Depression and the decline in wheat farming, a result of the ravaging Dust Bowl, times were hard all the way around. Most folks who dug in—and didn't move to the city in hopes of a better life—struggled to get by. The Coons had it rough, too, but fared better than most rural families.

As Delbert made his way to the pond that day with the horse, he knew to keep his eyes peeled for snakes. When he and his brothers weren't busy with their daily chores, they could be spotted shooting chicken hawks or catching water moccasins unawares; they'd zero in while the snakes sunned themselves on the branches of the willow trees. Then they'd aim their .22 rifles and shoot them dead.

So he was expecting snakes, but he wasn't expecting to happen upon two strangers—a man and a woman—kicking back on the banks of the family's twelve-foot deep pond.

He was curious, so he stopped near enough to converse with the couple, letting the horse lower its muzzle to the cool water. The twosome had spread a blanket under a stand of oak trees where buttercups dotted the grass. Out yonder was a peach orchard as well as pecan and pear trees. It was a lovely place to stop. The teen couldn't really blame them. He glanced over and gave them a nod. The man, clad in a dark single-breasted suit, wouldn't look straight at Delbert, but the woman seemed friendly and she smiled.

"Is it okay if we rest here awhile?" she asked, motioning with a delicate hand. She was a cute woman, young and petite, but she looked a bit travel worn.

Delbert slid his flat newsboy cap back and scratched his head. "No harm in it, I don't reckon," he said.

To his right, he caught sight of the couple's gleaming Ford Coupe. They had parked off the gravel road, snuggled up close to the bushy bodark trees that lined the road's edges. From there they would have had to climb through a barbed-wire fence before making their way to the pond.

"Well, I better git for home," Delbert said, as he tugged the lead and pulled the horse's head around. He didn't really give the pair much thought as he turned and led the horse back to the barn.

It wasn't until a few days later when he read a feature in the daily paper with photos of the very couple he'd spoken to that Delbert made the startling connection. The duo parked on their farm that day had been two of the most hunted gangsters in Texas, and now they were wanted for another murder. Their names were Bonnie Parker and Clyde Barrow.

Clyde and his pretty sidekick fronted a small band of outlaws called the Barrow Gang. The dire economic and environmental conditions of the dirty thirties proved to be the ideal breeding ground for the deadly and ill-fated duo.

This little coterie of criminals boldly and haphazardly plied its trade during the time of the big-league gangsters like John Dillinger, Pretty Boy Floyd, and Baby-face Nelson. What set this band of luckless gangsters apart, however, was that a sort of outlaw version of Romeo and Juliet was at the helm. But even Shakespeare couldn't have dreamed up all the crazy, nerve-wracking, and tragic misadventures the lovers would bring upon themselves and those who stood in their way.

Clyde Barrow led the gang, but with his spritely moll—who the public came to perceive as his trigger-happy dame—they captured the imagination of a nation. Other gang members played less prominent roles in the ever-changing saga, including Clyde's older brother, Buck, who had a young wife named Blanche.

During Bonnie and Clyde's two-year plunder across middle-America, they would frighten, shock, disgust, entertain and beguile the masses; their luck would finally spin itself out on a lonesome dirt road in northeastern Louisiana.

Chapter 1: A Love Bigger than Texas

Bonnie Parker and Clyde Barrow took their first struggling breaths almost twenty months apart. Although they started out in different parts of Texas, destiny would step in and bring them together. But before that could happen, nineteen hardscrabble years stretched out like a long dusty road between them.

Clyde Chestnut Barrow shot into the world on March 23, 1909. His parents, Henry and Cumie Barrow already had four small mouths to feed, and more would follow. Now they had a family of seven, including five boisterous young'uns, crowded into their wee hovel of a tenant shack. Unbeknownst to them, worst living conditions lay in store.

A weary Henry inspected the squalling infant he held up in one hand. Another boy, he thought proudly. But pride went only so far for a man who could barely provide for his family. The downtrodden patriarch tried to remind himself of the extra farmhand he'd have down the road.

Through the years, Clyde proved to be more of a curse than a blessing to his family, but love him they did.

As a boy, Clyde admired his older brother, Buck. The older boy may have been nicknamed after the fleet-of-foot deer family, but he behaved more like a wily coyote, looting hen houses early on. Soon Buck graduated from hens to turkeys and from turkeys to cars. And every time Buck swiped something, he whittled away a portion of his conscience.

In lean times, many a poor man turned to gambling, in one form or another. Farmers gambled every time they planted a crop, not knowing if there'd be rain enough for growing. The only gambling Henry Barrow ever wagered in, outside of farming, took place on a racetrack. But the thundering hooves of the bangtails only left him empty-handed, with a heart full of ache and head full of useless dreams.

It's no surprise then that Buck had a gambling streak as well—but he had a bloody, cockfighting gambling streak. Henry made a feeble attempt at talking some sense into his boy, but once Buck got a taste of money in his pocket, the feathers flew again and again. Then, somewhere along the line, he got hold of a pit bull, a real bone-polisher. Buck went from cockfights to dogfights to fist fights and from one woman to another, until he met Blanche Caldwell.

Clyde studied his older brother's maneuverings. He also sat in the picture shows, taking in every exploit of the wild west outlaws. He rode alongside Billy the Kid and fled in a hail of bullets with the folk hero Jesse James. The bigger-than-life screen idols mesmerized the poor scrawny kid from the plains of Telico, Texas, beckoning him, daring him to follow suit.

He only had a few years of formal schooling under his belt, but Clyde proved to be an apt pupil—at least of the outlaws. He imitated their criminal ways and played the part well during carefree childhood games. But make-believe bullets didn't hurt, and nobody ever keeled over dead from a stick gun and a thin-throated, "Bang, bang, you're dead!"

Carefree days existed more in imagination than in reality, at least for the Barrow kids. Preoccupation with growling stomachs and the pinched-up worried faces of their luckless parents put a damper on innocent fantasies. Relocating from one measly farm to the next, and then dwelling in a tenement camp on the wrong side of Dallas, forced them to grow up fast and tough.

Back when Clyde still waddled around the barnyard in bare feet and a saggy diaper, the future love of his life was born in Rowena, Texas. It was the first of October 1910, and, needless to say, she delighted the eyes of her parents, Emma and Henry Parker. Four years later Henry died from an unknown illness. This loss may be why Bonnie clung to Clyde Barrow to the bitter end. It's also why her mama moved her fatherless family to Cement City, ever closer to her daughter's eventual soul mate.

Bonnie excelled in school but married an immature young man named Roy Thornton when she was only sixteen. Her pick of a husband left a lot to be desired. Not only did he abandon her for another woman as soon as he grew bored, but he also ended up behind bars thanks to his sticky fingers. Though she became weepy without him, her love for him never compared to her eventual feelings for Clyde Barrow.

As a young woman with few viable skills, Bonnie settled for waiting tables in a café. She knew how to lead men on to garner bigger tips, and sometimes they wanted more than a refill on coffee—if she ever obliged them, she kept it to herself. She'd rather live a glamorous life, but working and being around people lifted her spirits somewhat—until she lost her job. So did 4.8 million other

Americans, and Bonnie's melancholy returned. She wondered if this was all life had to offer and wished something exciting would happen and whisk her away from her dreary life in Cement City.

At last the stars aligned in a blissful yet fateful way in the winter of 1930.

The Barrows had moved to west Dallas and, after years of camping out by the Trinity River, Henry and Cumie finally got a place of their own. It was a humble filling station with meager living quarters in back and tall thin gas pumps out front. On the roof Henry hoisted huge signs that read HB BARROW, Star Service Station, and Coca Cola.

Never one to let a good time pass him by, Clyde attended a shindig near his folk's place around the first of the year. Once there, his eyes immediately gravitated toward a little spit of a gal. He learned her name was Bonnie, and he was determined to have her by his side.

Clyde had charisma and a boyish charm, almost an innocent presence, which counteracted the antisocial side forming behind his smile. He was immediately taken with Bonnie: her looks, her size, and her flirtatiousness. Nineteen-year-old Bonnie had a way of gaining favor with those around her; she was scrappy and feminine all at once. Perfect for him.

On her end the attraction was mutual. Though Bonnie hadn't divorced her wayward husband (and never would get around to it), she finally found her prince charming in Clyde Barrow. Bonnie simply swooned over him.

The two were a magnetic couple and couldn't keep their hands of one another. He would hold her by the slender waist and tell everyone what a dandy she was. Her confidence was appealing, and physique-wise she was well put together. What she lacked in outstanding beauty she enhanced with makeup, which she applied lavishly.

One day Bonnie might wear her bobbed hair pinned up or tucked under a close-fitting Cloche hat. The next day she might wear her fair hair in a soft finger-wave style, and she'd sport tiny round stud earrings, dainty like her. Her long curly upper lashes, brushed with mascara and perfectly separated, framed her big misty eyes—blue eyes that looked like pearls in the rain. She painted her lips with a flair that accentuated their curves, shaped like the top half of a heart. Her slender build and 4'11" height made her every bit as petite as Clyde's mama.

At 5'6" and 125 pounds, Clyde could feel tall standing next to his little lady. Bonnie adored his cute dimples and elfish ears. His narrow nose, with a bit of a down-turned tip, was skewed slightly to the right, the kind of characteristic that adds interest—at least to the more careful observer—and Bonnie memorized every inch of Clyde Chestnut Barrow, every little idiosyncrasy, every move of the head and slight of the hand. She stared into his penetrating, coffee-colored eyes, studied his every expression, his every mood. She grew to know him in ways no one else could. His thin upper lip and pouty lower lip often appeared pursed, as if set in defiance. He had a nice hairline and slightly arched brows, the kind a girl would trade her virtue for. In a mugshot four years earlier, he'd stood and raised his left eyebrow slightly, not consciously aware, really, just giving a look of, so you think you can tie me down, huh?

He would soon be posing for another mugshot—just two short weeks after meeting the love of his life. Throughout his teens he'd been hauled in numerous times on suspicion of car theft or attempted burglary, but he'd never suffered the humiliation of being cuffed in front of a girl he'd fallen hard for, let alone in front of her mother.

The one time Bonnie's mama invited him to sleep on their couch, he behaved like a perfect gentleman, trying to impress the unimpressible Emma Parker. But the Dallas police got wind of his whereabouts and gave him a buzz bright and early the next morning. Groggily, Clyde pulled himself up and stumbled to the door only to feel his heart sink when he saw who stood before him. Not again, Clyde thought. The deputies let him pull his shoes on before they led him out the door.

Bonnie ran into the room in a panic. "It's alright, Baby girl," Clyde said over his shoulder. "I'll be out in a few hours; wait for me."

But Clyde wouldn't be out in a few hours. He wouldn't even be out in a few days or a few months. Somewhere in the big state of Texas, two hearts hurt to be together: one very lonely young lady, who was once again waitress-bound, and one very scared young man riding the chain to the putrid hellhole called Eastham Prison Farm.

Chapter 2: Incarceration

Even at sixteen Clyde had been cocky—with a twinkle in his eye and a slight smile on his face—when he was cuffed and printed on the third of December 1926 for auto theft. The guard behind the camera that day had clicked the first mugshot, then he threw Clyde in the caboose and locked the steel door, but the charges were later dismissed due to a lack of evidence. Then on February 22 the cops hauled him in again for similar crimes, this time in Fort Worth. These charges were also dropped.

Now, after his arrest in front of his girl, Clyde hoped for another dismissal. But he had warrants from numerous counties hanging over his head—and he wouldn't be released from custody until each warrant had been addressed. He was spirited from Dallas County to Denton County and from Denton to McLennan County. He lucked out in Denton County and skated by on attempted robbery charges, but when the deputies transferred him to McLennan County, the law finally hit pay dirt, sentencing him for numerous offenses including car thefts. They nailed him with a two-year sentence, but it could have been a lot worse. Still, two years was too long for a free-roaming, lovesick thief.

While he waited to be moved from jail to prison, his mind kicked into gear, and so did Bonnie. She immediately came to his aid, writing love letters and promising her complete devotion. She waited anxiously for Clyde's jailhouse letters, and the yearning intensified. She visited him in the Waco jail whenever she got the chance, swearing she would wait for him.

But he didn't plan on being transferred to any prison and feared that he would be warehoused at the dreaded Eastham prison farm. He would rather be locked away at the state prison in Huntsville, where Buck was currently doing time for his own robberies. Clyde had to find a way to break out of county before the authorities sent him to the farm.

Clyde's cellie, William Turner, had just the plan in mind. All they needed was a gun.

Bonnie had it bad for Clyde, so it didn't take much on Clyde's part to coerce her into saving the day. She clearly had a wild streak, and it would take just a little nudge to push her over the edge.

All she would have to do, according to Clyde, was pull a break-and-enter into Turner's parent's house, find a handgun hidden there, and become a mule of sorts, smuggling the pistol into jail under her dress. Clyde made sure she knew that he loved her to pieces and that she was the sweetest honey in the world.

She made up her mind and stepped into her new role as an accomplice, playing the part as if she were Greta Garbo. She'd always dreamed of becoming an actress; now she'd get the chance to try out her skills and act calm in front of the jailers while her heart fluttered like a captive bird in her chest. She had to make it look like just another innocent visit, and somehow she pulled it off.

The jailbirds made their move on March 11, 1930. After Clyde and Turner recruited another person named Emery Abernathy, they came up with a ruse to lure one of the deputy jailers to the cells and then switched places with him at gunpoint. The trio made their break and hoofed it down Waco's Sixth Street, dodging another lawman's bullets as they disappeared around the corner. It wouldn't be the last time Clyde Barrow danced on blacktop during a getaway.

Once the fugitives got out of county they went on the run, and Bonnie waited nervously for word from them. Clyde had his demons, but for better or worse, Bonnie loved him. She'd taken a big risk helping him, but before they even had a chance for a romantic reunion, the police apprehended him—over a thousand miles away in Middletown, Ohio.

After that the judge ratcheted Clyde's two-year term up to a fourteen-year sentence. Right away a frantic Cumie Barrow went to bat for her wayward son, appealing to the governor for help. As for Bonnie, her letters tapered off a bit after Clyde's demoralizing recapture.

From April 1930 to February 1932, Clyde faced his darkest days. One bright spot during this time was meeting Ralph Fults, a fellow inmate and escapee. They were being transferred from county on the same day to the prison farm for hard labor. Fults, who'd done a bit at Eastham before escaping, was on his way back and was sure to pay dearly. Together, their steel bracelets clanging, they shuffled into the chicken-coop-like truck with the other inmates for the dreaded ride to Eastham. Clyde picked Fults' brain about the notorious facility like a young soldier heading into the front lines of battle for the first time.

Once housed at the work farm, Clyde's monotonous daily routine started with a meal that could barely keep a mongrel alive. Then he filed in behind Fults in the work line with hundreds of other inmates. He'd been assigned to chop wood alongside Fults.

Stepping from the din of the prison each morning to the blinding sun and the stark white outer walls of the cement prison was a jolt in itself. Clyde often looked longingly into the distance where the flat land stretched for thousands of acres to the edge of the vast blue sky, and he longed to be free again, to roam, to do as he pleased. But there wasn't time to dally and daydream. The guards—many on horses back—watched the prisoners closely, forcing them to move out on foot at a rapid clip. Like the other inmates, Clyde worked ten or more hours a day in all kinds of weather or faced a thrashing.

One day he was forced to witness the guard's brutal retaliation against Fults for the prior escape. Clyde stood feet from the beating, wanting to spring to his friend's defense, but the guards had the bulge on Fults, and there was nothing Clyde could do. He seethed on the sidelines, every muscle tensed to explode, vowing that he'd make them pay. Someday, someway they'd pay.

Clyde experienced his own drubbings at the hands of the guards, but he also suffered at the hands of brutal inmates. Eventually he took action and hammered a guy who'd buggered him in the barracks. The rapes went on for nearly a year as murder grew in Clyde's heart. He had it all planned. He only needed a minute, two tops, to do the bastard in. Before Eastham, he'd never killed anyone, but now someone had pushed him too far.

The older inmate, Ed Crowder (or Big Ed as people called him), saw Clyde as a pretty boy, someone he could easily overpower and have his way with. Crowder, a bank robber serving a fifty-year term, was also a sexual predator. Six inches taller than Clyde, he outweighed him by 70 pounds. And he was right, he could overpower Clyde, but he underestimated the wiry little guy's resolve. And that mistake cost the creep his life. He died in the midnight hours after receiving over two-dozen stab wounds, back in the shadows of the prison showers. Aubrey Scalley, another robber doing fifty years, willingly took the fall for Clyde. But it was common knowledge around the farm who the real killer had been.

Killing Big Ed did not solve all of Clyde's problems. It got to the point where he couldn't take the spirit-crushing life at Eastham anymore. Like other despondent inmates, who employed self-injury as a means of escape—to at least get off work duty or get transferred to a better institution—Clyde devised a desperate plan. He chopped wood and had access to hatchets, so he made up his mind to use one on himself. Whether another inmate helped him, he wouldn't say, but someone swung that ax, chopping Clyde's big toe off in one fell swoop. Part of Clyde's second toe went with it. Clyde screamed like never before as his legs gave out beneath him, and he grabbed his bleeding left foot in his hands as the scenery swirled around him. He felt sick, faint, and had to focus on breathing while the guards made their way to the newest victim of their harsh regime.

If only Clyde had waited.

Cumie Barrow had been feverishly working to get her boy released. Thanks to overcrowding and a governor in a generous mood, her phone calls and letters finally paid off on February 2, 1932. Clyde was released a week after sacrificing his toes, not because of the injury but because of his mother's efforts.

Freedom was a miracle, but Clyde had become acclimated to the subculture of prison life, and it had hardened him. After Eastham, the sparkle dimmed in his eyes, and he made up his mind that he'd never be taken alive again, never be locked up and tortured again no matter what. But Clyde still liked to have a goodtime. He lived for a good time. He lived for money. And he lived for revenge—revenge against the guards at Eastham and revenge against anyone who tried to take him down.

Chapter 3: Early Misadventures and Murders

Clyde may have lived for retaliation, but he also lived for Bonnie, and the first thing he did upon release was woo her back. "I'm sorry, Dollface," he purred, "I missed you something awful." He kissed her tenderly and buried his face in her cottony hair. She smelled like soap and powder, and he never wanted to let her go.

That's all it took. She kissed him passionately as if he'd never been gone. Two years apart had done little to melt her desire for him. Had he not been on crutches he would have picked her up and twirled her around. He might limp like a three-legged dog now, but he'd always been a little rough around the edges anyway, and his spunk endeared her to him.

Clyde may have been dizzy with a dame, but absconding with other people's possessions ranked high on his list of priorities. Young Mr. Barrow didn't borrow anything. He took it. And right now, he needed a car. He scouted around and spotted a shiny new flivver, a V-8, with its key stuck temptingly in the ignition. He tilted his wide-brimmed fedora down low over his right eye. Then, like a copperhead eyeing a swamp rabbit, he picked his moment and slithered up close. With lightning speed, he moved in undetected and slipped into the driver's seat, popped the clutch, turned the key, shifted into first, and sent his new wheels reeling down the road. He threw a look behind him. No one chasing him. Good! He hated it when that happened.

In spite of his lawlessness, Clyde's family remained loyal to him and he to them. Family visits became a tricky affair as his crimes piled up, but he often managed to sneak in and see them without being spotted by cops. To his parent's dismay, Clyde Barrow was one young man who would never be a farmer, neither would he be a low-wage factory worker or construction worker or any other kind of underling in any form of legitimate employ. He'd given working for a living a half-hearted try, and it hadn't worked out for him. He wasn't wired for it. Besides, anything too regimented reminded him of prison. Not only that, but he couldn't hack being ordered around.

After reuniting with Bonnie, Clyde formed a small gang that included Ralph Fults (who'd been released from Eastham ahead of him) and another ex-con named Raymond Hamilton. Fults was his first pick because the guy knew how to hold his mud and could be trusted to watch Clyde's back. But he needed a third shill, so he recruited Hamilton.

Early on, when Clyde had an angle to work in town, Bonnie stayed behind while the Barrow gang pulled the job. And they wasted no time diving into crime. Safecracking had worked well in the past, so Clyde agreed to another box job, this time at an oil refinery. All they needed was the right can opener and the payroll would be theirs. Unfortunately, their timing was off, and they had to tie up some unexpected workers only to find out the safe was bare. Three weeks out of prison, Clyde was off to a bad start.

Other robberies followed. Sometimes they'd barely make off with nothing. Other times they'd do all right, a few hundred, maybe a few thousand if lucky.

One month after becoming a free man, Clyde took Bonnie along with him and Fults. After stealing some cars, the trio stopped in Kaufman, Texas, a small town about thirty minutes outside Dallas. That's where Fults got the big idea to break into a hardware store and steal some guns.

They pressed their luck, and a keen-eyed security guard caught them in the act. Clyde and Fults hightailed it down the street and Bonnie jumped out of one of the hot cars, darting after them. Gunfire cracked the night air, and Fults took a bullet in the arm. They kept running. After spending a miserable night hiding and working their way slowly on foot in a downpour, the law cornered them. Clyde, ever determined to avoid prison, escaped in a rain of bullets, leaving Bonnie and Fults behind to get arrested. He'd worry about breaking them out later if necessary.

Now it was Bonnie's turn to sit in jail waiting to be tried for attempted robbery. To help her cope, she turned to writing poetry, for which she'd always had a knack. Clyde's gangster lifestyle heavily influenced the subject of her poems.

Eleven days after the fiasco in Kaufman, Clyde felt antsy and decided to take a poke at a store in Hillsboro. With Bonnie and Fults behind bars, Clyde recruited a couple crooks named Ted Rogers and Johnny Russell. He told them it would be easy. It wasn't. In fact, before going through with it, Clyde started getting cold feet, due in part to the jitters from the hardware-store debacle and the fear that the storeowner's wife there in Hillsboro might recognize him. Rogers and Russell, dead set on moving forward, cajoled him into helping; he agreed but said he'd wait in the car.

While he waited behind the wheel with the motor running, hoping the duo didn't blow it, a gunshot startled him. He gripped the steering wheel. . . *come on, come on, get out of there*! He revved the engine, ready to bolt. Finally the others came tearing out the door with guns and goods in hand. Clyde hit the gas before their doors even closed.

He swerved around a parked car, "What the hell happened?"

He didn't really want to know that Rogers had laid the shopkeeper out. Bucher hadn't given him any choice, pulling a gun on them like he did.

"Christ! Why'd you bump him?"

"He didn't leave me no choice!" Rogers said, trying to catch his breath and holding up a wad of jewelry.

Jewelry and forty bucks—forty lousy bucks! Traded for a man's life. It was an all-time low. Clyde had no choice but to take his share of the loot and split.

It didn't take a genius to figure out that Clyde would get the electric chair if he was convicted of murder. He'd always gotten along just fine without electricity and had no desire to make up for lost time. Besides, he'd already made up his mind back in Eastham: he'd die where he stood before he'd ever be arrested again. The only electricity Clyde needed was the current that buzzed between him and Bonnie.

Miss Parker's trial finally got underway on June 17, 1932. To her great relief she was acquitted and once again tasted the air of freedom. Neither her stint in jail nor John Bucher's murder dissuaded her from being with Clyde. She was in deep water, and instead of swimming to the safety of shore, she allowed the dangerous current to pull her further out. Even in August, when another innocent man lost his life due to the Barrow Gang—in a festive atmosphere during an Oklahoma barn dance—she ignored the red flags waving in front of her lovesick eyes. Clyde had been one of the triggermen this time, taking the life of Sheriff Eugene Moore. Bonnie's dependencies and her attraction to bad boys created the right combination to reel her further in.

Clyde reeled in a teenager named W.D. Jones, too, on Christmas Eve. He put him to work right away, stealing a Model A Ford. Bonnie decided to go along with them, and what was supposed to be a low-risk crime to get W.D.'s feet wet turned into murder. The car owner, Doyle Johnson, pursued the thieves as they got the car rolling, and in the heat of the moment, Clyde shot Doyle, who had grabbed him through the window. All that over a car that would now have to be discarded a few miles down the road. Bonnie followed in another Ford, playing her part as an accomplice in the deadly scene.

Not long after the Christmas murder, more chaos loomed in Texas. As usual, Clyde was trouble; it didn't matter where he went, something bad was bound to go down. This time he, Bonnie, and W.D. rolled up to the home of Raymond Hamilton's sister. Unbeknownst to them, the law had a sting operation stationed there in an effort to catch Grapevine Bank robber Odell Chambers. By the time Clyde realized the place was crawling with cops, he'd already approached the house. With his ever-present sidearm that he had slipped inside his waistcoat sleeve, he fired indiscriminately, killing Malcolm Davis, a deputy sheriff and a handsome man with a thick mop of wavy hair.

After this latest murder, the threesome became chronic wanderers, wearing ruts into the back roads of No Man's Land. Clyde peered out the car window at a mountain of dust on the horizon. Two days quiet, now this. He coughed and rolled up his window. The landscape of the Great Plains stretched out before them, flat as a frozen pond, and brown, except where drifts of fine silt had swept up around fence posts and tractors, plows and barns. Everything was brown. They passed homes where exhausted women swept brown plumes of dust out their doorways, shaking it from rugs and clothes and children's hair. The roads wore the color of dirt too, and the Barrow Gang drove endlessly, never staying in one place long, trying to outrun the dust storms and cops that were always closing in.

When reality started closing in as well, Bonnie tipped back a flask of whiskey to help numb the pain—the pain of the lows that lived between the highs, those heightened moments when their senses kicked in, when all their nerve cells fired and adrenaline pumped through their blood. Time afforded no self-pity when they were fleeing a scene at breakneck speeds. Always the ultimate rush.

Clyde's crimes didn't bother her so much as the not being able to close that door at will and open the one that led back into her old life. But there was no going back now. She had crossed that line riding shotgun—and every lawman in Texas had Clyde's name on a shiny new bullet.

Chapter 4: Buck Joins the Barrow Gang

Clyde's older brother, Buck, spent fifteen months behind bars at Huntsville for robbery before being granted a hard-won pardon on March 23, 1933. Upon his release, he assured his wife, Blanche, that he would earn an honest living. Prison, he promised, had cured him of his criminal ways.

The older Barrow was a few inches taller than Clyde and had a thin face but heavier eyebrows. He couldn't be described as handsome, really, but he did have what some women might consider a beautifully chiseled chin. He dressed in dark suits, occasionally pinstriped, and loved to cut it up with people in photos—like his male cousin. He would pretend to hold the man at gun point and force him to stand with his hands up, and then Buck would pat him down with great authority. But the older Barrow lacked the charisma of his younger brother, Clyde. After prison, Buck's hairline receded slightly, but Blanche considered him to be the cat's meow, and he adored her.

He loved running his fingers through Blanche's pretty black hair, which she wore about chin length. Sometimes she styled it in a Marcel wave, but in the months following Buck's release, she left it naturally loose and tousled. She had a handsome nose and chin, a small frame and shapely legs. Like other stylish women of her time she wore tidy, knee-length dresses or skirts that either fell softly along her curves or flared out in a girlish, flirty way. Sometimes she wore slacks. Very much the lady, she often wore heels with little bows on the straps, or she wore lace-up flats. Slim to begin with, she became terribly gaunt by the end of her Barrow Gang ordeal.

When the courts cleared her husband's criminal record, she was ecstatic, believing he would clean up his act. Exactly how he planned to suddenly change into an upstanding citizen in an economy that left millions bereft of employment was another story. Fresh out of the gate, the newly pardoned Barrow figured finding a job could wait. He deserved a vacation, after all, and wanted to hang out with Clyde and make up for lost time. Never mind that his younger brother was a fugitive on the run from the law—now wanted for murder.

Buck may have been a thief but he'd never knocked a man off before. Still, the whole time he'd languished in state prison, he'd been preoccupied with the trouble Clyde was in. Buck blamed himself for leading his younger brother astray.

Blanche wanted to spend time with her husband more than anything else in the world but had no desire to spend time with his gangster brother. She tried her best to talk Buck out of chumming with him, but Clyde was very persuasive and promised them both that he'd rent them all an apartment out of state, somewhere like Missouri, where they could lay low for a few weeks and celebrate.

When it was clear that Buck wanted to soak up his newfound freedom with both his wife and the Barrow Gang, Blanche acquiesced and went along for the ride. She'd already spent over a year waiting on daddy, she would say, and she wasn't about to live without him another day, not while he gallivanted across the country without her. It didn't hurt that Buck drove up in a new car that he had managed to acquire legally from an acquaintance. Blanche saw the title to the Marmon, their new luxury sedan, before Buck slipped the paper into his coat pocket. She made up her mind to make the best of the trip. Then she and Buck could come back and start their wonderful life together at last.

She couldn't have been more wrong.

The plan was simple. The married couple would hook up with Clyde, Bonnie, and W.D. at a motor court in Oklahoma. From there they would caravan to Joplin, Missouri for their holiday. Aside from the fact that Buck pulled into the wrong motor court in Oklahoma, the Marmon had one problem after another: flat tires, leaky oil, knocking engine, even a leaky radiator. If the car trouble was some kind of omen, it wasn't heeded. As fate would have it, the couple hooked up with the Barrow Gang and rolled through Oklahoma behind Clyde's latest stolen Ford V-8.

The mood was jovial. For hours the two-car caravan rolled along, through wheat land ravaged by drought, past abandoned farm houses, past Model T trucks loaded down with tables and chairs and mattresses, tin buckets and dirty-faced children. The Barrow clan roared past these destitute families, some broken down on the sides of the highways, many part of the great exodus to California or some shantytown along the way. Finally, Clyde finally pulled over to sleep for the night.

The group spent a few layovers in tourist courts en route to Joplin, always careful to keep an eye out for nosey hosts and locals. All Bonnie and Clyde needed was for some Oakie to recognize one of them from a newspaper photograph. If that happened, the whole night's rest would be ruined, and they'd be forced to pack up and move on. As it turned out, the travelers went unnoticed, and they enjoyed the use of electricity, kitchenettes, showers and beds.

At last, on April 1, the quintet made it to Joplin. For the next couple weeks they would all have a home base and an address on 34th street. Their rental unit was a blocky, white-rock, two-story apartment. Downstairs, a spacious garage granted Clyde the perfect opportunity to hide his Ford. To the left of the garage, a long staircase led up to the two-bedroom apartment that sat directly above the garage. A two-week stay sounded like heaven to Bonnie after being on the run for so long.

Everyone helped unload the luggage, which included suitcases, Clyde's guitar, Bonnie's red makeup case with its gold clasps, her poetry, and the gang's lethal freight—several rifles, a pocket pistol, a revolver, and Clyde's weapon of choice, a Browning Automatic. Buck wasn't packing, but Clyde wore iron everywhere, even while praying.

What household items they didn't have they purchased in town. They all made a cozy little hangout, with everything they needed to make the place comfortable. Clyde and Bonnie took the bedroom in the back. That left the master bedroom on the street side for Buck and Blanche. W.D. slept quite comfortably in the living room when the group bothered to sleep at all.

Night after night the five vacationers partied, played cards, worked jigsaw puzzles and took full advantage of the recent lift on prohibition. They spent their days resting, followed by another night of laughing, eating, gambling, tipping flasks and pitching woo.

The nights also provided good cover for robberies. At first Clyde and W.D disappeared alone to fatten up the bankroll. Buck didn't turn the money down, but he tried to convince his brother to reconsider. Unfortunately, Clyde refused to listen.

In the mornings the sun tried to shine through the windows, but Clyde kept them covered at all times. Blanche drank less and rose earlier than the others, cooking and cleaning long before the last of the stragglers climbed out of bed. By then the days were half over. The clan's odd hours and nighttime outings didn't go unnoticed. Certainly, bad news followed the Barrow boys around, and Joplin was no exception.

# # #

"Hey, watch this!" Clyde said, motioning for Buck and W.D. to look up and take notice. "This bean-shooter can fire twenty rounds into a guy before he knows what hit him."

The three men had driven into the Missouri countryside to target practice. Clyde had talked Buck into breaking into a military arsenal where the government had stored a horde of weapons after the war. The brothers helped themselves to a host of Browning BARS. Loaded, the men needed to test-fire their new stash.

They acted like kids on Christmas morning, all giddy and proud of their shiny new toys. The first few guns fired straight; then the next one jammed. They put that one aside. Clyde picked up another one. He fixed a magazine into the weapon and ran the receiver. Then he aimed at a road sign and squeezed the trigger. The noise was deafening, and the gun kept firing and firing and firing, making a dreadful racket; it wouldn't stop.

"Lay off the trigger!" Buck shouted.

"I ain't touching it!" Clyde hollered back. Bewildered, he stood holding the gun away from his body. He stood half bent over because he couldn't quit laughing. "Stand back! I'm gonna throw it in the creek." Clyde heaved the gun over the bank and they all ducked.

The plan worked.

"Whew!" W.D. whistled, "That was a close one, Boss." He walked closer and peered into the creek. "For a second there, I thought you was gonna lose another toe."

"Boy, you best close your head before I close it for you," Clyde said, in mock annoyance.

The three laughed all the way back to the apartment. Of course they had to have a few drinks on it once they got there, reliving it for Bonnie and Blanche, who hooted like they'd been dipping into the giggle juice all day.

On their last day in Missouri, Clyde steered through the streets of Joplin with W.D. riding along. They left the Ford at the residence and were in another bent car, a Roadster that W.D., like a good little gopher, had hiked on the day before. They needed some travel money before the group could head out of state.

Clyde gave him the low-down. "Okay, listen, Boy. I'll go in and wave my pistol in the clerk's face. You wait behind the wheel."

Clyde turned down a side street and glanced behind them to see if anyone followed.

"Look," said W.D., pointing at the engine. "She's smoking."

"Awe man, that don't look good," Clyde said, punching the steering wheel. "We fried the motor." He made a U turn. "Let's head back."

The women waited in the apartment, Bonnie nursing a hangover and Blanche packing suitcases, preparing anxiously to get out of Dodge. The guys promised they wouldn't pull any jobs, but they'd gone back on their word. Now Blanche had an impending sense of doom and worried that the law would close in on her and Buck before they could separate from Clyde and the others.

Blanche's intuition was right. The law was on the road and heading their way. It was April 13, 1933—a turning point for Buck and Blanche—one they could never turn back from. The honeymoon was about to end.

The cops had the element of surprise on their side. It would be five lawmen against five penned-up partiers. What the cops didn't know was that the five staying in the apartment had firepower on their side—and at least one gangster who had the electric chair propelling him to pull the trigger.

To their own detriment, the Texans had tallied a few hours too long. Once on the road they could have outrun the heat, but, instead, they would find themselves trapped. None of the Joplin lawmen knew their group was cornering the Barrow Gang. They each just thought they had some run-of-the-mill car thieves who probably had a stash of contraband—booze and what have you.

Buck had been working on the Marmon that afternoon, changing its oil and tinkering, getting it ready for the ensuing road trip. Upstairs, Bonnie sat in her nightgown (even though it was 4:00 p.m.) trying to rhyme away her self-induced headache. She wanted to revise a poem she'd written in jail.

She heard the roadster return and the garage door open. She decided to put away her poetry and see about pulling the job with Clyde and W.D. They couldn't be done already.

All of the sudden both women in the apartment—and the whole neighborhood for that matter—heard what sounded like machine-gun fire. Blanche squawked and Bonnie jumped up in her slippers and grabbed a gun.

Before the gunfire erupted, Clyde had stepped from the fried Roadster to close the garage door behind them. Just then he heard another car whiz into the driveway. Buck took a look. "It's the law!"

Startled, Buck and W.D. dove for guns. Clyde already had one.

Before Clyde could finish closing the garage door, a man slipped through the opening. Clyde disengaged his gun at point blank range, and Wes Harryman, a startled lawman, slumped to the cement floor, a warrant in one hand, a pistol in the other. *Dumb sucker.* Clyde turned the gun to the street and all hell broke loose. Bullets shot in and out of the garage windows. Glass flew through the air and a bullet plowed clean though W.D.'s gut. Another lawman, Harry McGinnis, was hit several times, his arm left mangled and hanging by a thread.

"Let's scram. *Now!*" Clyde yelled. Bonnie and W.D. scrambled into the Ford. Someone would have to shove the cop's car out of the driveway. Harryman, the first cop to go down, lay in the way too.

A quick look. The guy was chilled off, but they couldn't stomach driving over the body. Clyde shot a look through the garage-door window, "Help me drag him out of the way." Buck and Clyde worked fast. Then Clyde ordered Blanche, who had run down the stairs, to help him shove the cop car down the driveway. More gunfire erupted from the street and she bolted, screaming for dear life.

Miraculously, everyone made it into the car, even Blanche. The three remaining lawmen—seeking shelter behind trees and cars—watched in disbelief as the crowded Ford hurtled down Thirty-fourth Street and careened around the corner to the right. The whole incident took place in a flash, leaving the ink on Bonnie's poem nearly as wet as the blood pooling on the garage floor.

Buck glanced behind them. "I've been clipped!" He said through clenched teeth.

"Oh my God!" Blanche screamed. "Are you hurt bad, Daddy?" Blanche kept screaming; she was losing it something awful.

"Close your yap, Blanche!" Bonnie yelled.

All three men got lead poisoning that day. Clyde took powder in the chest—it stung bad, but the buckshot could be dug out later. Right now the pummeled gangster had to focus on driving like hell. One of the lawmen had fired a rebound bullet that had thwacked Buck hard in the chest but failed to penetrate. And then there was W.D., who had the more serious wound.

Clyde drove like a maniac, making good headway, enough to pull over in the woods and attend to W.D. The boy was moaning, crying that he was dying, thinking the bullet had lodged in his stomach. They dragged him out of the Ford and spread him on the ground.

Clyde snapped a thin branch off a tree while the others knelt over W.D. Then Clyde wrapped the end of his crude medical instrument with gauze and told W.D. to lay still. After poking the stick slowly into the wound, they all helped to roll him partway over to see if the branch would come out the other side. It did.

"You got daylight showin' through your belly, Boy." Clyde stood up and peered down the road, anger and grit creased in his face. "Come on, let's dust out of here," he said.

Buck helped slide W.D. into the backseat with the women, shoving guns and crap out of the way. Then they covered him with a blood-soiled sheet and tore down the road. There was only one thing to do: snatch a doctor's bag from a car near a hospital. At the first opportunity, they did. Then, at their next makeshift roadside stop, they had morphine tablets and syrup, syringes, clean gauze, and bandages.

During the mad dash for freedom, bullets had rained down. Now the sky began to rain down, and the dirt roads became slick with mud. Mud and gunk and fear, and at their feet, blood, mostly W.D.'s. It sloshed back and forth on the floorboards of the car and mingled with the smell of stale gunpowder and fresh rain. And the miles poured on hard.

Everything they had, short of a few guns, they had abandoned back in Joplin. All their clothes, their bedding, Clyde's guitar, the camera, film. Gone. But no one mourned the loss of their belongings more than Blanche. All the hopes she'd held in the world were back at that apartment: proof of Buck's clemency, proof of their marriage, proof of their car ownership, everything. But the only proof that mattered to the law was the proof that she and Buck had been involved with Bonnie and Clyde, during robberies, a shootout, and two murders.

Now the men who'd likely shoot her and Buck on the spot were pawing through her purse and other personal items. It was more than she could bear. With every racing mile, through darkness on into dawn, she and Buck's dreams, or what was left of them, disappeared into the roiling dust.

Chapter 5: Platte City Wakeup Call

The Joplin shootout left all of their nerves frayed. The gang embarked on a harried and exhaustive sojourn that led them first to Shamrock, Texas, then to Amarillo and on through numerous other towns and states in an endless cycle. The days all blurred into one and time lost its meaning. Fights broke out between Bonnie and Clyde, between Buck and Blanche, and between the two Barrow brothers. Altercations were nothing new, but now they took on a heightened ferocity.

One day, when temperatures rose to an all-time high, Bonnie and Clyde went at it. "Break it up!" Buck ordered, pulling Clyde off Bonnie. But Bonnie lurched forward and clobbered Clyde again, screaming at him. The squabble rattled everyone to the breaking point but eventually wore itself out. A while later, Bonnie and Clyde started hugging and smooching and it was "Doll" and "Baby girl," and "Honey, I love you."

Sometimes the brothers got into brawls while the Ford barreled down the road. In one such incident, they argued back and forth, Buck challenging Clyde's authority. They couldn't agree on anything. Then the yelling started. Clyde pasted Buck good upside the head. Then Clyde took a right hook right and that did it. He grabbed the nearest gun and stuck it in Buck's face, fuming.

Buck backed down.

While the Barrow Gang found themselves in one uproar after another, the whole nation was in an uproar over a large batch of photos the outlaws had taken. The authorities found rolls of film in the Joplin hangout and immediately processed them, distributing the photos to newspapers and True Crime publications. The snap shots provided captivating insight into Bonnie and Clyde's rebellious spirits as well as their life on the road with their entourage.

Before Buck and Blanche hooked up with the threesome, Bonnie and Clyde had acquired a camera. It was a Kodak Brownie Box camera that they toted around in a nice hard-shell case. While Bonnie and Clyde posed in front of the Brownie, W.D. stood behind the lens, snapping many of the infamous pictures.

Of all the things Bonnie and Clyde acquired during their extended crime spree, their camera became the catalyst that pushed them into the national spotlight. At last, the public could get a glimpse of the outlaws in action, to see them standing alongside their stolen motor cars, guns at the ready. Bonnie and Clyde built their images around their Fords and firearms, which also served as status symbols for a band of hoodlums that—besides their flair for style—had little else to flaunt.

One snap shot showed Bonnie pretending to disarm Clyde, holding him at arm's length while aiming a shotgun at his chest. Clyde had tilted his hat back in a boyish manner, and his dimples gave him away—he looked at her a little wearily, a little lovingly, obviously amused by her prank. He sat on the front bumper of a car in another photo, displaying two firearms (nearly as big he was) across his lap. Both Bonnie and Clyde had an actor's flare, adding to the intrigue spreading from city to city.

For one photo, Bonnie stood with her hands on her hips and two pistols tucked in a belt around her thin waist; she wore a light-colored blazer over a form-fitting skirt that day. She often wore the same Mary Jane shoes, high heels with a thin strap that she buckled around each ankle.

One photo in particular churned the rumor mill into full gear: Bonnie stood with a fat cigar in the right corner of her mouth and a pistol at her hip. She looked tough, seductive, and dangerous. Standing in front of the Ford, she leaned forward slightly, with her left elbow resting on a headlight. She propped her left foot up on the front bumper and jutted her elbows out to either side, like spread wings, similar to the flying goose radiator cap hood ornament to her left.

Other photos illustrated the love the brothers felt for their women. Buck sat on the runner of a car in one print, wrapping his arms around Blanche, who was seated on his lap. Bonnie and Clyde stood arm in arm in another photo, looking very much the sweethearts they were.

All in all, the more surly snap shots boosted the gang's notorious image in the public's eye. There was no doubt that they were desperate and dangerous and on the move. As their infamy grew, Bonnie Parker became the trigger-happy starlet riding shotgun alongside the dapper and dangerous Clyde Barrow. He dressed like the gangster legends of the silver screen, but he was the real deal. In reality, he and the others became increasingly rumpled and dirty from life on the road.

They solved their wardrobe dilemmas easily enough. They either purchased new digs with stolen money or had them laundered in town while they cooled their heels a safe distance away. Serious injuries, however, weren't so easily alleviated.

The gang's address was the open road (and the not-so-open road when they hit washouts or cattle drives). On the one hand, life on the run was the ultimate freedom. On the other, it was a self-imposed prison with no walls.

After spending several weeks wheeling down dusty back roads, the group headed to Florida. They became sun worshippers for a few days before Clyde and Bonnie got spooked and bolted. Buck and his flame enjoyed the surf and sand so much that they stayed on, but Buck got too drunk on the beach and people started staring. Blanche tried to talk some sense into him, telling him to hush up and to stop bringing attention to them. Buck stumbled on some driftwood and shooed her away. Then he took another swig of hooch and burped like he had a bullfrog in his belly.

Blanche stood there in the sand in her v-neck one-piece swimsuit and hooded beach wrap, looking every bit the pretty young wife whose husband had gotten lit and was running off at the mouth. If people only knew who they really were, she thought, they'd either clear out or close in.

In June, after visiting Blanche's father, she and Buck headed to Oklahoma to meet up with Clyde and the others. On the way there, Buck lost control of the car on a curve. The wipeout rendered their current vehicle useless. Buck spent several hours trying to find another car to steal while Blanche waited alone in the woods with their gear. He finally found a V-8 coupe and returned to retrieve his bruised wife. Thankfully, neither she nor Buck suffered any serious injury in the accident. In a few days, Bonnie wouldn't be so lucky.

The ninth of June started out way too hot and would end in one of the worst ways possible. Clyde had a habit of driving too fast. Everyone knew it and accepted it. His driving had gotten them out of so many tight spots that they trusted his judgment behind the wheel. But a fine car, like a good horse, needs to be respected. One mustn't get too comfortable around either. Clyde got too comfortable well after dark near the town of Wellington, Texas.

He didn't know the road they were traveling. He also didn't know he had missed a detour sign and that there was no useable bridge over the river ahead. The Red River was running low, but its banks were plenty high—high enough to get a car airborne and flipping over several times before coming to a jarring stop on its side.

A farmer named Sam Pritchard and his son saw the whole thing and wasted no time heading down their driveway to the scene of the accident. Clyde and W.D. suffered injuries. Clyde broke his nose and W.D. got banged up pretty good. They pulled themselves out of the wrecked car, but Bonnie was seriously injured and temporarily trapped, long enough to suffer severe burns up and down her right leg. She had taken a blow to the chest as well. Battery acid ate through her leg, boring into muscle and exposing bone.

Meanwhile, Buck and Blanche wondered what had happened to the others when they didn't show up on time. They decided to hang around for a while longer.

At the accident scene, Clyde worried about Bonnie, he worried about the car, and he worried about the arsenal of weapons still in the mangled heap in the riverbed. The Pritchard men carried Bonnie up to their house to have the womenfolk tend to her.

After seeing Clyde pulling guns from the wreckage, Prichard's son-in-law slipped away to summon law enforcement. George Cory showed up with another lawman, Paul Hardy. They intended to take control of the situation, help the injured woman, and deal with the men and the guns. But the men with the guns took control of them instead, forcing the two of them into the backseat of their own car. Then Clyde took the wheel, while W.D. held the cops at gunpoint. With Bonnie on board they set out to meet up with Buck and Blanche.

Later on, the Barrow brothers tied the officers to a tree. The lawmen would live. Bonnie's life, however, still hung in the balance.

After the accident, Clyde and the others treated Bonnie, changing her bandages and applying salve. But Bonnie would never walk normally again.

On July 18, 1933, Clyde pulled into a motor court near Platte City. The disheveled clan needed a rest, but they should have avoided taking one there. On the plus side, they could order food and booze from the Red Crown Tavern, and they could send Blanche over to the well-stocked store that doubled as a cafe, to pick up food. And lastly, they had access to a filling station when they were ready for the next leg of their journey—at Clyde's discretion of course. But for now they could rest.

After the newcomers settled in, the locals started standing around pointing toward the cabins, gathering in huddles like they were gossiping about something everyone but the Barrow Gang was privy to. Buck and the others had noticed it a little but seemed preoccupied with nursing Bonnie and needing a break from the road. Denial set in like a welcome breeze on a sultry night. They filled their stomachs and slipped into bed. For the most part, they all slept about as soundly as a watchdog after a tussle with a grizzly bear; but another night of sleeping in the cars would have been worse.

The sun rose like any other summer morning, and the day was a repeat of the previous one. Blanch did most of the footwork, since people might not recognize her as easily as the others. She padded across the parking lot feeling more frightened and blue than ever. As she approached the Red Crown Tavern, she noticed the customers talking and moving about animatedly through the screened-in door, but when she opened it and stepped inside, a hush fell over the room. She felt the weight of all eyes upon her, as if she were an alien from Mars. She felt sure they were on to her.

When she purchased the day's food, she spoke so softly that the clerk had to lean forward to hear. Blanche fumbled with a pocketful of stolen coins that Clyde had thrust into her hands, and she couldn't wait to get the heck out of there.

After she returned to the cabin, lugging an armload of food, no one took her worries seriously, especially Clyde. He and the men had broken into another armory, and they had enough guns for a small army. Guns gave Clyde a sense of invincibility that Blanche didn't share. He insinuated that Blanche was just being paranoid.

Blanche looked down at her food and frowned, telling them not to blame her if things went down tonight and none of them saw the light of morning.

After supper, they retired to their separate cabins and crashed for the night.

If Blanche had stayed there alone, she may have sailed by without raising suspicion, but with the bulk of the group holed up in the quaint cabins acting sneaky and unsociable, it rubbed a burr in the cockles of the locals. It's not surprising, then, that Holt Coffey, the local badge, was given a heads up.

While they slept the second night, the heat wave was bearing down.

Coffey had taken the chatter seriously and had rounded up an impressive group of men. He also rounded up some powerful firearms and a fortified car. The lawmen gathered quietly, waiting until well after the bewitching hour to make their move.

Clyde woke with a start, quickly processing the sounds—not normal nocturnal sounds but terrifying sounds, sounds of someone banging on a door, someone revving an engine real close—too close, and now voices, a commotion.

He jumped out of bed and swung his roscoe around letting it rip through the cabin window. W.D. fell in alongside him. Violence exploded from the other cabin, too, and return fire erupted immediately. The deafening noise continued unabated as W.D. grabbed the keys and ran from the cabin to the garage, through an adjoining door, to start the Ford. Clyde may have thought they could tear out of the garage and plow through the shooters, but he didn't expect an armored car to be blocking the garage. He focused like a surgeon, emptying his BAR into the driver's side, hoping the driver would get the hint. He did. After the bullets penetrated the steel-plated car and tore through the driver's knees, the injured man quickly moved the beast out of the way. The horn was stuck in the on position, adding to the pandemonium.

Buck and Blanche still had to make it to the car but could only make it to the garage through their front door. They had no choice but to make a run for it through the deafening noise. When they did, a bullet slammed into Buck's left temple. Blanche saw him go down and ran to his rescue, pulling him up and dragging him to the car.

Once again, Clyde floored it and bulldozed through a wall of gunfire. That didn't stop the gunmen from pummeling the Ford with bullets. Some of the glass fragments from one of the car's windows flew into Blanche's eyes, nearly blinding her. She held Buck, sheltering him, clinging to him like never before.

The lawmen watched in amazement as the gangsters escaped their dragnet, but they had scored big hitting Buck in the head. Clyde hauled ass while Buck's breathing grew shallow. For now Clyde had to keep rolling, even though one of the tires was blown out. Bonnie held her leg, while Buck bled out in Blanche's lap and darkness swallowed the battered Ford into a maze of Missouri back roads.

Chapter 6: Dexfield Park

After Platte City, the hopeless rabble hightailed it out of Missouri and ended up in Iowa. Clyde started looking for a place to set up camp. Holing up anywhere was risky, but with Buck so close to death, there was little choice. They needed to do what they could for his head wound, even if it was just to pour rubbing alcohol in it and bandage it up. Besides, Clyde was finding it difficult to focus on driving and Bonnie needed her burn tended to.

The fourth of July had come and gone, leaving none of them in the mood for celebrating. They'd seen enough fireworks in Joplin and Platte City already.

Clyde ended up parking in a wooded area on the outskirts of a deserted amusement park. It had closed down for want of business half a year back. The park, once a bustling playground for happy families, lovers, and tourists, was now a place of refuge for a desperate band of criminals.

Clyde and W.D. set to work immediately, pulling seat cushions out of the car for Buck and Bonnie to rest on. Blanche remained close to her husband, comforting him, trying to hear his heartbeat whenever he got very still. He hadn't died yet, but another hour or another day would take care of that.

Clyde stepped away with W.D. "He's not going to make it," Clyde said, shaking his head and looking around.

"What should we do?"

Clyde took a deep breath, "Dig a grave."

Awhile later, Clyde helped Bonnie into the bullet-ridden car for a supply run. It was a huge risk, venturing into town, but they needed bandages and ice for Buck, ointment for Bonnie's burn, clean clothes, food, and a different car.

When he and Bonnie returned, Clyde gathered an armload of wood scraps and started a small fire in a clearing on which to burn bloody bandages and clothing. Next, he lit a campfire near the car for roasting hot dogs.

It would prove to be a long, spooky night, with owls hooting and shrieking and swooping in low overhead. If only the group had taken this as a warning and cleared out. If only. But it was not to be. They stayed put, spending an eerie and restless night beneath the stars where dread lived in every shadow and fear in every snap of a twig. Not a one of them forgetting that they could be attacked at any moment.

Blanche fought sleep all night, holding Buck and straining to hear the faintest of heartbeats, the shallowest of breaths, waiting while the life of her husband slipped away. "Don't fade on me now, Daddy," she whispered, the tears spilling from her injured eyes. She could make out light and movement, but the shards of glass had compromised her vision.

W.D. had seen all the action he cared to see. All he could think about was how to get out of the mess he was in. Blanche had encouraged him to break away, reminding him that he was young and might be able to salvage some semblance of a life. But would he live through the night?

Clyde slept in fits and starts, knowing that Blanche would stay awake and watch over Buck. They all dreaded the moment when death would reach out of the shadows and snatch him from them.

They had good reason to be frightened. Between the burnt remains of bandages in the woods and Clyde's hefty purchase of medical supplies at the drugstore, locals started taking notice. They shared notes and put two and two together. The first whispers of gossip built into a crescendo of voices that grew to include the sheriff and the chief of police. From there, other officers joined the wave of lawmen and vigilantes, all well aware of the Barrow Gang's recent shootouts. Even Iowa's Bureau of Investigation got involved.

The desperados had been raided in broad daylight in Joplin, and in the middle of the night near Platte City. In Iowa, the newly formed posse, too numerous for a quick headcount, had decided to strike the desperados at daybreak.

Clyde awoke in the misty morning hours, feeling relieved that hoot owls rather than lawmen had harangued them during the night. He sensed nothing of the danger lurking in the woods. He wanted to hit the road early, though, so he and W.D. restarted the campfire and busied themselves cooking breakfast.

They never had the chance to eat it.

The posse had crept as close as they dared. When they got within five or six motor-car lengths away, Clyde turned with a start.

Whether he fired first or the cops fired first, somebody was going down. An effusion of gunfire exploded from the trees and exploded from Clyde's autoloader. W.D. felt searing pain in his hand, chest, and calve before he even had a chance to grab a gun. But he still went for it, getting nailed by bullets and buckshot and machine-gun fire in the process.

Clyde kept shooting in the direction of the lynch mob, trying to hold it back while yelling at W.D. to start the engine. Meanwhile, Bonnie dragged her bad leg behind her as she scurried to the Ford. Buck and Blanche fell in behind her, struggling for the tenuous safety of the backseat.

When Clyde saw W.D. fumbling around behind the wheel, he took over, even though he had a serious gunshot wound to the arm. He didn't do much better. The car hurtled forward, but Clyde slammed on the brakes as soon as he realized he'd hit a dead end. He whipped the wheel around and road up onto a stump that caught in the undercarriage, forcing them all to throw open the suicide doors and make a run for it.

Bonnie half ran and half limped with the help of W.D. while Clyde provided cover with a barrage of bullets. The trio fought their way through the brush along the Raccoon River and scuttled down the banks.

After running out of bullets, Clyde accessed the situation. Bullets still zinged by them, torpedoing into the water as the trio huddled at the river's edge. Bonnie had a superficial gunshot wound to the stomach, which added to the mixture of blood flowing into the water. Then the shooting let up and Clyde decided to scout out the area on the other side.

"I'll be right back," he whispered.

Bonnie and W.D. watched him wade across the river and clamor up the opposite bank until they lost sight of him. He sprinted a ways, keeping low and holding his injured arm, until he spotted a farm. He turned back for Bonnie and the boy.

Somehow W.D. managed to follow Clyde and help Bonnie across the river. The trio came out the other side soaking wet and bleeding but determined to find a car. Clyde still had his empty gun and brandished it at the farmer and his family before making off with their Plymouth.

Back across the river, Buck and Blanche hunched in behind a log. The posse had broken into two units, one of which was bearing down on the terrified couple. Buck fired his gun a few times only to meet with a new stream of bullets that tore through his body, jolting him like a rag doll next to his horrified wife.

"I'm done for, Baby." He gasped. "Please go find the others. Don't worry about me."

Blanche refused to listen, convinced life without Buck was no life worth living. She wanted to be shot when Buck died, but so far, she was the only one who hadn't been hit.

Then she started thinking about Buck dying there in the dirt with even more bullets blasting through him. She hollered, "Don't shoot!" And she threw her arms up in surrender; then she pulled Buck up on his feet to prove he no longer held a gun. The throng moved in like hounds on two wounded rabbits.

They made their arrests and hauled the injured criminals off for medical treatment. Bonnie saw Buck for the last time but heard that he had died in a bed, on clean sheets with his mama at his bedside.

Out on the road, three injured and bedraggled outlaws swapped the stolen Plymouth for a Ford, and where they headed next was anybody's guess.

Chapter 7: The Final Run

After the beating they took in Iowa, the three remaining fugitives fled through Nebraska. They stopped in Colorado long enough to learn that the law had them on their radar there, too. From Colorado, they drove all the way down to Mississippi, holding up small stores or gas stations along the way. They tried not to dwell on whether the sand in the hourglass was running thin; instead, they busied themselves with their day-to-day survival needs.

W.D. quit the gang in early September, going home to visit family before facing his inevitable arrest. A murder charge hung over his head, for which he received only fifteen years, due to his being a minor. He would still be a fairly young man at the time of his release. Blanche had been right, W.D still had a chance to turn his life around.

Alone again, Bonnie and Clyde found a safe place outside Dallas for a family visit. Bonnie, more than ever, needed her mama and her sister to help her recover from the trauma of the car accident and the shootouts. It broke her family's heart to see her in such a poor state of health, and she was grateful to them for their care and attention.

It did Clyde and his family good to reconnect, too, especially after Buck's death. Being in Dallas for a while also gave Clyde the opportunity to enlist some new gang members. He still held a grudge against Eastham Prison, where his ex-associate, Raymond Hamilton, was incarcerated. Raymond clung to the hope that Buck would break him out. Floyd Hamilton, Raymond's brother, wanted to help, too. He and James Mullen, a two-bit crook and druggie, hooked up with Clyde to discuss their plan.

At the scheduled meet up, the three men and Bonnie stood outside their cars. Mullen addressed Clyde, "Here's the deal," he said, "We'll plant two pistols under that old wood bridge out behind the prison. You know the one?"

Clyde leaned against his Ford and took a drag off a Lucky Strike. "Yeah."

"All you gotta do is park on that there back road by camp one and wait. Drive Ray and a few others out of there."

"When's this goin' down?"

"Tuesday morning," Mullen replied, shifting from one leg to the other. "Well, what do you think?"

"I don't like it."

"What's not to like? It's perfect."

"Only one road out."

Bonnie chimed in, trying to encourage Clyde to go for it; they could use Raymond's help robbing banks.

Clyde dropped his cigarette butt and snuffed it out. "Okay, we'll be there—early. Get word to Raymond."

Bonnie and Clyde sat in the getaway car surrounded by a fog so thick that it choked out the sun for miles. They waited, peering into the gloom, watching for any sign of the inmates.

"There they are," Clyde motioned with a nod of the head as he cranked the engine.

Six men came running through the fog, too many to stuff into the car, until one took off on foot. Inmate Henry Methvin climbed into the Ford's trunk, and the others squished in on top of each other inside the car, willing to bear the discomfort for the sweet taste of freedom.

After the prison raid, the Barrow Gang's new recruits included Raymond Hamilton and Henry Methvin. They started robbing banks right away.

Meanwhile, the prison breakout got the attention of Frank Hamer, who was once a Texas Ranger. The prison manager, Lee Simmons, hired him to hunt down the Barrow Gang. Hamer followed leads and stayed a few steps behind, determined to end Clyde's crime spree once and for all. He drove a car just as powerful and got inside Clyde's head, learning everything he could about the gangster and how he operated.

Early in the year, after helping to rob several banks, Raymond moved on. That left Bonnie and Clyde with Henry Methvin, who wanted to travel to Louisiana to visit his folks. Henry's folks lived in Bienville Parish, a place Bonnie and Clyde came to enjoy. No one seemed to bother them there, and Henry's dad, Ivy, seemed to welcome their visits. The couple got into a routine, heading out of state to pull heists and then returning to Louisiana to relax in the countryside.

Then April came, and the gang headed to Dallas for an Easter Sunday family visit. They cooled their heels all afternoon on a rural road outside Grapevine, Texas, not expecting any trouble on a holiday. Two motorcycle cops patrolling the area weren't expecting much trouble either. That's why they turned up Dove Road. to casually inspect the four door parked there.

The younger officer, just getting his feet wet, was H.D. Murphy. His mentor was Officer Wheeler. Clyde planned to take them hostage, but once Methvin started shooting that plan went all to hell. The gang won the shootout, leaving two dead officers sprawled in the dirt.

Bonnie had a white Easter bunny in the back seat of the stolen black Ford sedan. She had planned to give the bunny to her mother as a present. Though Bonnie wasn't happy about the shootout, she seemed more worried about the bunny than the bright red blood pooling on Dove Road and the two officers shot down without warning on a beautiful Sunday afternoon.

Ivy Methvin didn't like the direction his son's life had taken, and he would do anything to save his son from more prison time. If the law would grant Henry a full pardon, Ivy told the officials, he would set up Bonnie and Clyde in exchange. Not only was Ivy willing to double-cross the couple, but Henry himself said he would cooperate.

Bonnie and Clyde had no idea that their new gunman was going behind their backs to help plan their downfall. They preoccupied themselves with putting distance between the Easter Day murders and their own hides. Hanging out in Texas wasn't an option.

The Barrow gang hit the road again, robbing and killing along the way. This time two officers in a car approached the trio when they parked off a road in Oklahoma. Clyde and Henry exited their cars and shot both officers. They killed Cal Campbell instantly and took a bleeding Percy Boyd hostage. Boyd hadn't been seriously injured and Clyde eventually let him go.

Meanwhile, Frank Hamer organized a serious-minded posse and put in place the final stages of an ambush plan that would end Bonnie and Clyde's reign of terror.

Chapter 8: Death and Legacy

Planning an ambush took time, even though the ultimate goal would take only seconds to accomplish. Half a dozen posse members, hailing from Texas and Louisiana, had to coordinate efforts with the informant and with officials from various agencies. They had to do this without tipping off the targets.

Bonnie and Clyde were flighty, after all, and would bolt sure as the sun sets if they had any suspicion. With no time to lose, the posse picked a time and a place for the surprise attack, based on Ivy's speculation concerning the fugitives' habits. Henry's job was to find an excuse to separate from the fugitives without raising any doubt.

On Wednesday morning, May 23, 1934, the triggermen packed various rifles, along with sandwiches and beverages, up to the high brushy ground along Highway 154. This wooded area in Gibsland, Louisiana provided the perfect cover for the death trap. They told Ivy Methvin to park his logging truck off the road and remove one of the tires, that way when Bonnie and Clyde spotted him working on his rig, they'd likely stop to chat.

The gangster couple was driving a grayish Ford V-8, the last car they would ever steal. Ivy expected them to roll down the highway any minute now. He got into position by his truck, nervously peering down the road in the direction Bonnie and Clyde would be coming. He planned to dive out of the way, maybe under his truck, just as soon as he could, without tipping off the gangsters. What would they do to him if they lived through this? The thought just scared the daylights out of him.

When the posse spotted the Ford down the highway, Clyde was driving at a good clip. The lawmen peered through the brushwood, raising their weapons and waiting as the Ford drew closer and closer. No one breathed.

As expected, Clyde hit the brakes as he approached Methvin's rig. The Ford was barely rolling when Bonnie and Clyde heard one of the last sounds they would ever hear. Gunshots. The first shot blasted through the air, slamming through the driver's side door and was immediately followed by a horrendous barrage of bullets. Bonnie let out a blood-curdling scream, and the bullets kept coming, ripping though glass and metal, ripping through flesh and bone—for a quarter of a minute or more.

The day had been calm just moments before when Bonnie, who busily munched on a sandwich, had said, "There's old man Methvin." She raised her right hand slightly—the one with the sandwich—sort of pointing in Ivy's direction.

"Maybe he knows where Henry ran off to," Clyde said, pushing in the brake and pulling up alongside Methvin, but then he saw a vehicle coming in the opposite direction, so he started pulling forward.

Bonnie and Clyde both heard the unmistakable sound of a gun; it broke the relative quiet of the morning where only seconds earlier the whine of the Ford's motor could be heard. The bullet hit its target and slammed through the driver's side door, hitting Clyde like a freight train. He never had a chance to pour on the gas and escape. His right foot let up and the car rolled forward.

Bonnie screamed because she heard the gunfire, screamed because she saw Clyde slump forward, and screamed because a fusillade started pouring in on them. The deafening cacophony slammed like a hell bell all around them—and the God-awful pain, until silence replaced the horrific sound and darkness replaced the morning sun.

After the last bullet bore through the V-8 an eerie calm lingered in the air along with the gun smoke. The shooters had already moved out from behind the brush and were hiking cautiously down the hillside toward the stillness in the car.

It was over. Clyde Barrow came into the world first and he left the world first, followed seconds later by Bonnie Parker. Even in death the two bandits were side by side, Bonnie leaned lifelessly against Clyde who died behind the wheel, much as he had lived.

Within minutes, Deputy Ted Hinton, one of the posse members, took aim once again, this time with a movie camera, shooting gritty video footage of the bloody scene. He zeroed in on the car, the bullet holes, the guns, and the bodies. Then he zoomed in on the dash area to show how the lead had ripped large chunks of plastic coating from the big steering wheel where moments earlier Clyde had placed his hands.

Lawmen had walked around to the two doors on the passenger side, swinging them open toward the back of the car. There was riffraff everywhere, on the seats, on the floor, spilling out onto the ground: The men started pulling clothing and blankets out of the car, either dropping them in piles on the ground, placing them on the car's roof, or draping them over the top of the open doors. They leaned the shotguns up at the back of the car and gathered numerous automatic pistols and ammo. Newspapers littered the ground with stories about the couple on every front page.

# # #

Thousands of curious people flocked to view Bonnie and Clyde's bodies and to attend their funerals. Bonnie died in a dress, and in her casket she wore a light blue gown buttoned up to the neck, all signs of gore had been carefully washed away and her face covered with makeup. She looked serene and beautiful surrounded by cushions of antique-white satin. Her family refused to bury her next to Clyde.

His surviving kin buried him alongside Buck, not far from their childhood stomping grounds. The brothers began sharing the same headstone that day just as they had shared so much in life.

As the years passed, folks in Louisiana started organizing annual festivals at the ambush site and reenacting the events. People cashed in on the death car, too, taking it on tours around the country, so curious onlookers could stare in disbelief at the slew of bullet-holes in the body of the Ford. People purchased and fought over the couple's possessions, many items being resold at tremendous profits over the years.

Several books would be written and movies inspired by the lives of Bonnie and Clyde, but no one would ever quite bring back to life two of the most polarizing gangsters the country had ever seen.

Conclusion

In the wake of their deaths, the country continued to struggle through its darkest hour, but it forged ahead. The Barrows and Parkers forged ahead as well, and time began to heal the trail of wounds. People visited Bonnie and Clyde's graves and still would decades hence, but other graves existed, victims' graves, those gunned down by Clyde's bullets, while Bonnie reloaded guns or manned the getaway car.

Had it not been for the era in which they plied their trade, and the desperate conditions many Americans endured, Bonnie and Clyde may have ended up just two more malcontent miscreants, easily despised and easily forgotten. There would have been no monuments built, no books written, no movies made, and no songs sung about them and their notorious lives of crime. But instead, some portions of the public—who themselves wished to buck authority—held the outlaw couple up as anti-heroes. For better or worse, Bonnie Parker and Clyde Barrow lived and are remembered, not solely for the robberies they pulled or the murders they committed but for the love they shared. They were at times heartless, at times humorous, but always wild and reckless to the end.

Millions of people rejoiced when the Dust Bowl finally eased up, and all across America people returned to work at the end of the Great Depression. Grateful farmers once again set about planting successful crops, while implementing better soil management techniques. As time marched on, those unforgettable events took their place in the annals of history, as did Bonnie and Clyde.

Many years after the gangster couple pulled off the road to rest by a pond in Tarrant County, the school district purchased the farm and buried it under concrete—still, somewhere in a ditch along the road or a waterway nearby, a cotton mouth slithers through a pool of water in search of prey.

Bibliography

Barrow, Blanche Caldwell. *My Life with Bonnie & Clyde*. University of Oklahoma Press: Norman, 2004.

Biography. "The Story of Bonnie and Clyde: Love and Death." http://www.naistv.com/a.bonnieandclyde.html.

―――. "Desperados Kill Two Officers." Boston Globe, April 14, 1933.

―――. "Eyewitness to Shooting Gives A Word Picture." Boston Globe, April 14, 1933.

Burns, Ken. "The Dust Bowl." A Production of Florentine Films and WETA Television. PBS, 2012.

Coons, Roy. Interview. Previous resident of Bedford, Texas during the years 1928-1946. His older brother, Delbert, discovered Bonnie and Clyde on their family farm. Unpublished. (Names changed for privacy.)

———. "Tales of the Gun - Gangster Guns." Classic History Channel Documentary Series.

Dallas Historical Society. "Dallas History Special Section: Bonnie and Clyde." http://www.dallashistory.org/history/dallas/bandc.htm.

Guinn, Jeff. *Go Down Together: The True, Untold Story of Bonnie and Clyde*. New York: Simon and Shuster, 2009.

Jones, W.D. "Riding With Bonnie & Clyde." *Playboy Magazine*, 1968.

Klein, Christopher. "10 Things You May Not Know About the Dustbowl." 2012. *http://www.history.com/news/10-things-you-may-not-know-about-the-dust-bowl*.

Phillips, John Neal. "Running With Bonnie & Clyde: The Ten Fast Years of Roy Fults." University of Oklahoma Press: Norman, 1996.

Schneider, Paul. *Bonnie and Clyde: The Lives Behind the legend*. New York: Henry Holt and Company, 2009.

Timewatch: "The Real Bonnie and Clyde." Season 30, Episode 3 (7 Mar. 2009) TV Episode - 45 minute - Documentary.

Printed in Great Britain
by Amazon